THROUGH OUR EYES

Building a community for special needs families

Michelle Mandolene

BALBOA.PRESS

A DIVISION OF HAY HOUSE

Balboa Press books may be ordered through booksellers or by contacting:

Balboa Press
A Division of Hay House
1663 Liberty Drive
Bloomington, IN 47403
www.balboapress.com
844-682-1282

Because of the dynamic nature of the Internet, any web addresses or links contained in this book may have changed since publication and may no longer be valid. The views expressed in this work are solely those of the author and do not necessarily reflect the views of the publisher, and the publisher hereby disclaims any responsibility for them.

The author of this book does not dispense medical advice or prescribe the use of any technique as a form of treatment for physical, emotional, or medical problems without the advice of a physician, either directly or indirectly. The intent of the author is only to offer information of a general nature to help you in your quest for emotional and spiritual well-being. In the event you use any of the information in this book for yourself, which is your constitutional right, the author and the publisher assume no responsibility for your actions.

Any people depicted in stock imagery provided by Getty Images are models, and such images are being used for illustrative purposes only. Certain stock imagery © Getty Images.

Print information available on the last page.

ISBN: 979-8-7652-3306-1 (sc)
ISBN: 979-8-7652-3307-8 (hc)
ISBN: 979-8-7652-3308-5 (e)

Library of Congress Control Number: 2022914988

Balboa Press rev. date: 09/16/2022

Contents

Acknowledgments

My thanks and appreciation goes out to all of you who have helped me in this wonderful life. Thank you isn't enough to express the love and gratitude I feel for you.

To my son Tyler, for being so strong and patient and allowing me to be your mother, I am honored to call you my son. I have loved you pre birth and will post life. I love you to the moon and back.

To my daughter Ashley, for being the bright light and positive reinforcement I need daily. I am also honored to call you my daughter. "You are my sunshine" forever and ever. I love you to the moon and back.

To my twin Jodi, for never asking the "why" questions and for always sticking by my side no matter how hard life got. For stepping up to the "parent" role for my children. I know I can always count on you. You know my thoughts before I say them. We have a rare connection not many people understand or accept. We will always be together no matter how many lives we share. I love you Tootsio.

To my parents, thank you for making me the strong, determined woman I am today. Thanks for your love and support.

To my niece and nephew Lauryn and Ian, for your undying love, and support since you were born. For giving my children best friends for life and for giving us the laughter we so desperately needed in our lives.

To my brother Nathan and his family, Jen, Jasmine, and Austin, for supporting me with laughter and understanding. Thank you for supporting us.

To our Paula McGuire, thank you for your words of wisdom and purl retha of knowledge. We could not have done any of this without you. Keep learning and sharing, the world needs you.

To Andrew Kempleton, thank you for your wisdom, experience, and undying compassion to help my son.

To Patti Iwer, thank you for your wisdom, experience, and understanding of my son's physical, and emotional needs.

Finally to God, my loved ones who have passed, and our guardian angels. Thank you for always watching over us and guiding us. Thank you for encouraging us in the right direction and fulfilling our daily lives with your support. Thank you for encouraging Tyler and always being there for us.

Introduction

I have been in the health field for more than 30 years, starting when I was just 13 years old being a home health aide. I went on to college for Psychology, Occupational Therapy Assistant, and Dental Assistant. I worked in group home settings with Mentally Ill and Developmentally Disabled Individuals working as a counselor and Assistant Manager. Each life I live, I dive deeper and deeper into the health field, learning and experiencing along the way. My bright star gift is compassion and understanding. A giving heart with a thirst for knowledge in health care.

I thought all my experiences to date would've helped me with my children, but I was wrong, completely wrong. First with my daughter's life threatening nut allergy and then with my sons' diagnosis of Autism. I guess no one is really prepared for these things. The struggles and triumphs I've had along the way are what have made me the parent I am today.

I was always searching for a way to make my life easier like reading and researching. Teaching my children some sign language helped to reduce meltdowns and taught them patience. My daughter and son are 18 months apart. Quiet the challenge trying to breastfeed my son while my daughter was yanking on my finger to come and play. The disappointment of drying up and having to try 5 different types of formula before both my children were satisfied. The guilt started early on as a parent. My daughter didn't speak until she was 3. The doctors refused to test her at 2 years of age saying she'll be fine. At 2 ½ years old I insisted on an evaluation. My speech therapy friend taught me some exercises that I learned and modified them to benefit my daughter daily. By 3 years of age I couldn't shut her up, LOL. At the same time my son was screaming nightly for an hour at a time, every two hours and I was still at 4 hours of sleep a night. My son and daughter played together and my son didn't need speech therapy (he had 30 words by 12 months). I decided to be a proactive mom since my daughter had a speech delay. I thought, maybe I should see what my son knows. If I didn't have to teach my daughter speech I would've never really known how many words my son had at 12 months of age, and then how many he lost by 18 months of age.

My friend completed a developmental test on my son and we found out he was 9 months delayed so I started doing occupational therapy on him 3x's a week. He only continued to lose all ability to speak and point, prompting me to call an agency to come out and give him an evaluation at 22 months of age. He was diagnosed immediately and our world changed. Over the course of the next 15 years I continued to learn and educate myself since my son had so many health issues including several teeth and ear issues(4 ruptured ear drums and 17 ear infections since he was 9 months).

I do not regret any of my degrees because they have to this day, helped me extensively with my son. When I talk to therapy's, nurses, and doctors they treat me with respect (for the most part). I have always done 6–8/hour day training on food sensitivities, vitamins, modalities, etc, and will continue to learn going forward. With all of this experience I have, not much has changed in the health field regarding disablities. Yes the continual growth every ten years of new and improved discoveries, but I'm not talking about that. I'm talking about how the world perceives disabilities and how it/people haven't adapted. The world expects the disabled individuals to just "fit into" their world, but no one really understands. There are still stories from mothers saying when their child has a meltdown in a store on lookers come over and judge them telling them to parent their child. I feel this is completely unacceptable. What these mothers need is for a kind person to offer help not condescending comments and judgement. Unless you have a special needs child you really can't understand the complete exhausting we go through. I'm asking for people in this community to please help each other out.

This book is only some of my knowledge and experiences from the last 37 years. My hope is that you will read this book and take in my knowledge and understand I went through all of this, maybe just like you. That we, the people/parents, have to make a change and not expect the world to change. As you continue to read you will see some changes that I believe need to be made, which is why we need this intentional community to support our special needs individuals. I know there are many, many, more suggestions we will need to make this community happen. Please read with an open mind and join me on this journey.

1

Intentional Community

I stand there in helpless mode watching my 18 month old son screaming and thrashing backwards as he pounds his head against the floor in the waiting room of the pediatricians office, for 15 mins straight with no help. Trying to soothe my son from his pain, begging for help, and getting no answers. Watching my son develop and hit all his milestones from birth just to lose it all in front of my eyes by the time he was 18 months old was the most devastating thing I've ever had to go through. Watching him speak no more, constantly streaming, thrashing his little body, banging his head against me and the wall, not playing with his sister, starting to stim, and going into the abyss, is not what this book is about.

I know as a special needs parent we all have our horror stories. I want you to know that no matter when or how your child became special needs, I understand your pain and frustration with judgemental people, doctors, and the government. I truly believe now is the time we have to come together and make a change for our families, ourselves, and our future families.

After COVID, I know many individuals want to make life more meaningful, and focus more on families and friends, not on working and materialistic things. I know there are people out there who truly want to make a difference in someone's life. I want my great, great, great, grandchildren to live in a world where there is support not judgement, safety not bullying or killings, love, understanding, and caring for each other. A world/community where people look out for each other and step up to do so. None of this videoing while bullies hurt, but more of people stopping this, and people open to change. A community where doctors and the health field change their approach to healing. A place where Eastern and Western medicine can intertwin and work together, not fight each other. There is a place where both these modalities can thrive! Where the care for the individual is more important than the almighty dollar.

This book isn't about bashing or blaming anyone and not about reliving the past, but embracing the future and making it what we need it to be. We need to ask ourselves how badly do we want this change? Do we still want things to stay the same or get worse. Because the path we are on, things will only get worse. We are brave enough to come together and make the changes we want and no one can stop us! Together, we can help each other and change what we want to see change. I am asking you to take this journey with me.

2

Self Care

One of the most valuable and important things us parents can do is self care. It might be the hardest thing to ensure that we take care of ourselves daily, if not weekly. I know the one thing parents don't want to talk about is the future and what will happen to our children when we are gone. Thus, it is so very imperative we incorporate selfcare daily in our lives now. I know, easier said than done. I have been trying to incorporate self care for years. As parents, we need breaks but as special needs parents, it's crucial that we get breaks. Typical families can often take it for granted that they can go to one another's house, have their children play and get a break. They can afford babysitters and they can get babysitters easier. They can even go to restaurants, concerts, shopping, etc with no worries. When you are single, living on the low end of the middle class income, with no child support, most of your money goes for medical costs for your family. Low to middle class income families don't have the "extra" income a month to pay a babysitter and go to a restaurant. Then there's the hardship. Who will babysit my child/adult and treat them right? My son is over 6' tall,

250lbs, big barrel chested, nonberbal individual with sensory processing disorder, who can be aggressive at times. I haven't found one person who's willing to put themselves in the line of fire for under $15-20 an hour. And yes, that's more than what I make. So many times we step back from frustration and just take on the 24/7 job and accept it.

There are so many of us parents who think we are in this alone. We should never feel this way. I want all of us to come together for a solution to help each other out. We need to be happy, understanding, and have a lot of patience in our daily lives, let alone live forever! I am asking for your thoughts, suggestions, and your ideas of how we can help each other out with babysitting. My suggestion would be a system where parents "trade" with each other weekly to watch each other's son or daughter. One day a week with a rotating schedule. There can be a google spreadsheet, which is live, and several parents on this list trading times and rotating schedules. This is just an idea but it makes sure we have one night Friday/Saturday/Sunday spent with friends and family and one day during the week for appointments and/or for selfcare. This is just an example of what I think would work to ensure we get weekly self care.

It's an understanding that you are trading your time. A system of charts would be set up in case someone gets sick another parent can step in. As well as this doesn't cost us one penny. This "trading" time is just a thought, but I need help from y'all to come up with ideas and ways we can help each other. Respite is wonderful but only when it helps out. In 2018, when my son was put on the respite waiting list he was number 7500. If I'm thinking realistically, he won't ever get it therefore, it falls solely on parents once again to help each other out.

When it comes to self care, as hard as this is, we need to make it a priority for ourselves. I believe doing something little every day will help your state of mind. Find a time 30–60 mins daily to do what relaxes you. I find that the first hour of my morning is the best time. My son takes that amount of time to wake up so I take advantage of that time. Yes I need to attend to my son's initial physical needs first, but I find it's the most quiet time and uninterrupted time of the day to focus on myself. It has taken me years to say "it's okay, I am worth it" and not have guilt. We give so much of ourselves. We feel no one understands or no one is going through what we go through or that we are alone. By ensuring a little bit of time daily to relax, it rejuvenates us to get through the day. I find once my day gets started it's go, go, go. After I bathe him, read to him, and put him to sleep, I am completely exhausted by the end of the day. I do find it hard to relax. Most of the time I just want an hour to do nothing, just mind numbing activities, like watch TV.

I have tried to limit TV watching to 3 days a week. The other nights I will meditate for 5-10 mins and/or my gratitude journal in my bedroom before bed. Something to calm my brain because the minute my body hits the bed it wants to sleep, but my brian says differently. It took my son until he was 10 years to sleep 7 hours straight and that's because I finally agreed to give him medicine.

I have found if I commit to this routine 15-30 mins before bed I fall asleep quicker. Everyone has their own thing. I just found that since the friends I do have, really can't relate and truly understand me (even though they try), meditation, stretching, manifesting, and journaling have helped me. I also write down 3-5 things that I am grateful for in this journal, as well as the feeling I'd like to feel in the morning when I wake.

I also ask my guides to remove any negative emotions/energy that I've collected throughout the day to be removed. I will sometimes listen to meditation or frequencies to fall asleep. Either way, these are some of the things I do in my daily routine to be grateful and start the next day on a good note. One extra thing I do daily, is when needed, I put a shield/bubble around me and/or my son when entering buildings or a car, as well as remove energy when we leave these buildings and or car. I really don't want anything else coming home with us. Especially a public outing or school. Lots of energy is collected at these places.

In the modalities chapter I have listed several types of therapies I have used over the past 17 years. Other forms of self care and therapies are working with Healers or Life Coaches, Transcendental Meditation, Reiki, Somatic therapy, OT, PT, taking epsom salt baths, reading, etc. You need to make you a priority in order to give your child/adult all that is needed for the day. Celebrate the little things you do and do this weekly. It doesn't have to be something big but it must be something that makes you happy or feel relaxed.

I have worked with an amazing energy psychologist, who has helped me in numerous ways. She helps me to have a different perspective on many situations. She has introduced me to several different modalities to help me cope with my extremely challenging life. She constantly makes me accountable for me. She never lets me rant and rave, keeping me in a calm state of mind (making me aware that I'm not calm). She's always reminding me "What are you going to do to celebrate this week", "What are you going to do for yourself"? We should always try to remember to celebrate the small things and party with the big things! Some modalities this healter introduced me to are: TAT, Theta, Tapping, Energy clearing and testing, muscle testing, flower essences, and more. I also speak briefly on these in the "Modalities" chapter.

In this community, I believe we need self care and we are willing to help each other out because we need it, but also because we know just what each other is going through and just how valuable our time really is. My vision for this community would have a zen garden to go to block out the world and revive us. A place of sanctuary to remind us we are worthy, we are human, we are important. Even having a zen garden to have business meetings/zoom calls, and group therapy, would be so beneficial for us parents, as well as other family members.

3

Public Venues

My son has severe sensory processing disorder preventing us from going out to all public places. We are only able to go to curbside for groceries, drive through restaurants, parks, and beaches. We are so limited making us feel more secluded and envious that typical people do what they want when they want. If we try to enter a store it has to be right when it opens and for only 20-30 mins, top. No lines, no people, hopefully no smells from the store and /or people. My son must wear noise cancelling headphones, which physically hurt the outside of his ears, and it took us four years before he would wear them. I have exhausted my search for a good pair of headphones and/ or airpods that my son would utilize.

When it comes to restaurants, they are crowded, and the music is so loud. If there is music it should be turned down not blaring so loud it's heard from the parking lot. The wait time for food is long, the A/C unit blowing on us is irritating, the judgmental stares, waiters and waitresses not understanding we need exactly what we ordered, quickly, and we needed the check when we walked into the restaurant. It would be amazing to have all restaurants with a menu that has gluten-free options and other Allergen options. This community needs to have restaurants, stores, and buildings that accommodate our children, not making our children "get through" an outing causing meltdowns and pain. I believe our children have the right to go out too so why shouldn't they? There should be an area for meltdowns, rooms to prevent a meltdown or help an individual going through a melt down. Maybe three to four rooms for privacy and necessary meltdown. A calm relaxing room, soft items so no self harm can be done, it has to be soundproof, with several deep pressure items to calm down, sensory items to relax, dim lights, tunnels to crawl through, bolsters, and organic non fragrant cleaners for staff to clean after use. No hand blow dryers in the bathrooms or loud flushing toilets. Room in every stall for 2 people (yes I have to take my son into the women's restroom into one stall and help him), and all stalls must be wheelchair accessible, not just one. Maybe even an area where elopers have a "space" to run around to release their anxiety in public settings would help out. When my son was an eloper I would have him and his sister "race" each other from one spot to another just to relax him. This would ease his anxiety and allow him to not feel trapped. My hope is that if we put certain things into place the elopers and meltdowns will be significantly reduced, making for a happier individual and experience.

Everything should be hanidcapp accessible. Isles, cashier lines, bathroom stalls, etc. I'm not completely sure what anyone with a handicap would need, except lower countertops and room for wheelchair accessibility, therefore I'm asking you to stand up and speak. Let me know what you need. I'm sure I'm missing something that you would like in public settings. As for amusement parks, all of the above need to be incorporated as well (shorter wait lines, no crowding in lines, etc) a space to get out of line to relax and come back to the same spot in line. Several water parks would also be a must for this community. My son craves water at all costs. There wouldn't have to be big swirly slides, just straight 45 degree angled slides. I went to a park in Canada and they had 5 of these slides next to each other which you could enter from each side making it quick to get on the slide and not waiting, but a fun ride for the individual. I couldn't get my son off these slides in Canada! Two hours later they had to close and we had to stop, LOL.

For doctors and therapy offices all would apply as well, with some additions. No long waiting in either room. Not making the individual go get weighed and vitals checked out then have them return back to the waiting room. Yes, this does happen at a very well known Facility in SC (it did happen to us and the nurses were extremely put off when I said no we aren't going back to the waiting room, this will cause even more anxiety). They think it speeds up the process, but in reality, it creates more anxiety to special needs individuals. A medical alert should show up describing needs, any needs and/or behaviors that the staff can take to make the experience better, from the front desk to the waiting room to the exam room, as well as for the doctor. Our family members all have "special" needs and staff should comply with these in order to make an extremely anxiety ridden situation more accommodating.

For example, my son is nonverbal not dumb. Please address him and speak quietly and let him know what you are doing to him before you do it, as well as trusting the parent! If the parent says "no he doesn't put the thermometer in his mouth, please use his pit". Then they should respect the fact that the parent knows their child. There is more than one way to do things. It's more important to get the result than to get the result their way and cause a meltdown or aggressive behavior. Most places have to be more flexible, understanding, and maybe come up with different ways ahead of time in their practice in order to make this a smooth experience. My goal for all medical professionals would be to treat all patients like they are people, make them feel important. This also includes the Doctors. If you tell the nurse and she sees it on the medical alert then the Doctor should be reminded of this before he/she enters the exam room. Everyone needs to communicate inorder for things to run as smoothly as possible. They should use two time slots when booking appointments so there is enough time for our all needs. My son's Dentist office always books two slots in order to give my son time and to not stress out another child. These are simple yet effective small little things that will help our family members. Of course having patience and taking time to wait for my son to spell on the keyboard to see what he is typing. I know everyone is rushed but we need to slow down. Put yourself in their shoes, wouldn't you want someone to take the extra 5 mins seeing what your questions are? Of course you would. I don't give automatic respect anymore until a nurse, or doctor gives it to my son.

This goes for ER/hospital staff as well. I'm going to ask again, please do not ignore my son. Make eye contact with him and treat him like a person. Doctors should have emergency slots at the same time daily, as well as keeping several of them open. We used to do this in the dental office I worked at. There will ALWAYS be an emergency therefore, any office should have these slots opened. When drawing blood there should be an option to use the numbing patch prior to blood being drawn. Yes it adds to the wait time by 20 minutes, but the area is numb and the blood comes to the surface making the draw much easier. We had our patients use this in the fertility office

I worked at. There are devices, equipment, and tools we can use to help individuals. Let's make an effort to use them.

I do know how ER's can be very busy, which means time there is longer, so I will give a little leeway regarding time. A doctor who takes the time to talk to my son does not ignore him as he is sitting there still and quiet (not aggressive in any way) and doesn't say: "My colleagues would be mad at me for saying this... "We aren't equipped to handle this" "You're better off going to the children's hospital where they have candy and games, and staff there to handle this. From now on you need to go to them and not come here". Yes this just happened to my son in 2022! Of course, we didn't go anywhere else. My son completed a CT scan and had his blood drawn for the first time in 17 years with no movement. The audacity and judgement of some Doctors still shocks me. A doctor who doesn't believe your child is having pain because he isn't thrashing all around or because he is nonverbal doesn't mean he isn't in pain. My son was under extreme pain which is why we were at the ER. My son has feelings and is a person. In this community I believe we need to have medical professionals who have compassion, understanding, patience, and respect for all individuals. We waited 4 hours that day and I had to leave the room 4x's to get the doctor, frustrated because every time I saw him he was chilling on his phone. I finally just took the IV out of my son's arm and left and yes I know I shouldn't have but it shouldn't take these extreme measures for anyone to listen to an individual.

There should also be no staff "training" conducted on special needs individuals. Meaning, staff shouldn't train other staff members how to use the beds or gurneys while special needs individuals are on them. Making them jerk up and down on the Gurnee while that individual is learning how to use the bed (adding more anxiety to an already stressful situation). Let's use common sense and ask the patient or the parent if it would be okay first. Although, I understand we need to train individuals, it may be best to wait to do training on a typical person that doesn't have anxiety.

Dentists should use lead aprons as a blanket and pillows as the headrest while an individual is getting their teeth cleaned. We need to create a room in offices as a "practice room" with rubber dental equipment and noise that mimics the noise at the dentist office, and x-ray equipment. This should be available for everyone to practice, practice, practice. Knowing what to expect, how loud it will be, and the equipment used would be extremely helpful.

As for OP(Operating Room) appointments (we have had 6 OP visits and will need at least 3 more). Pre-registration is a must! No waiting at all. Check in to the hospital via text and have a nurse come and get your child/adult and take them directly to their room, along with a parent. Complete vitals in their room or have the patient get vitals at their doctor the day before, if that is better for the patient. If a child has sensory processing disorder, the staff should know the parent will have to wear an ID bracelet. The staff members should not judge or get mad/irritated that a patient can't wear the bracelet. Soothing hallways and elevators to relax us as well as no echoing rooms. I'm calling on individuals with trades that can somehow make the announcement and the bell quieter as well as maybe paint soothing colours. The hospital's operating rooms should have mobile handheld Xray units not 1 stationary unit. This would ensure xrays to be taken if you can't get them at the Dentist office. No prep in the pre OP room where there is a bunch of commotion and loudness. Go to a small private room with a door where the anesthesiologist and the doctor enter at the same time and only for one time. The more people who enter that room the more anxiety that individual will have. Have a patient wait there until the OR is ready. If the parent wants to go with their child/adult to the OR room let them, unless they are causing more anxiety of course.

Taking medication to relax an individual is ok for some people, my son's anxiety would get worse during the hour while waiting for the drug to kick in, as well as this is more medications my son would have to take. It would be amazing if parents had a Zen room for the waiting room to help them with their anxiety. Like all distractions, they/it should be quick. The longer the patient is in the recovery room the more stressed out they are. The first OR experiences we had I had to sit over my son on the gurney and hold him down while he came out of anaesthesia. They wheeled us out of the room up the elevator and into his room. We have learned which meds to give him to keep him relaxed and not aggressive but what horrible experiences. There is no way at 17 years of age I could hold my son down. They would have to mummy wrap him and I refuse to let that happen, so thank God we figured out the medicine situation.

There should be a daycare for siblings so the parent doesn't have to worry about childcare for another child they have while their child/adult is in surgery. I truly believe in the same building or office PAs, doctors, therapists should know western and eastern methods in order to help parents make a better decision about treatment. At least have both of those medicines available for us to make the right decision, and do not judge us because we need the Western medicine for a surgery but we prefer to have eastern medicine to aid in the treatment from the surgery. In a perfect world western and eastern medicine respect each other. In our/this community they will. There is place for each medicine working together that will ensure healthy individuals and quick recovery for all, if they choose. This is about what is best for your child/adult and they have a right to choose what method they want. There should be brochures for eastern and western medicine in all practices as well as the staff should ask the parents which way they would like to treat their child (with no judgement). All staff members should be trained as to how to handle meltdowns, to follow the parents' que, and be very respectful of special needs individuals.

4

Schools

There are several things that need to be changed in schools. One of which is the cafeteria food. I think all types of foods should be offered, especially healthy foods. I do understand most of our children are extremely picky eaters but nuggets, pizza, and macaroni and cheese shouldn't be the only thing offered. For my son, GFCF diet is what he needs to stay on, therefore these types of foods should be offered as well. Served at a different end of the line as to not cross contaminate. Any foods with nuts and peanuts should also be served in another area. We certainly don't want anapholatic shock with our children. Having cafeteria staff that is concerned and vigilant to make sure our children don't get the "dangerous" foods should be insisted. My daughter went through this first hand when the entire cafeteria staff didn't care that she has a nut allergy and served her food with nuts. The staff member who allowed her to buy this food (my daughter was 5yrs old) said "huh oh well" as she shrugged her shoulders. The cafeteria staff in the mess hall had no idea as to who my daughter was and what to do in an emergency situation. Since the Red Cross hasn't come up with a universal sign for anaphylactic shock there is no way of knowing when a child is raising their hand for a medical need or simply a napkin.

Therefore, all staff should be trained in epipen use and know the difference between a nut and a peanut, as well as who has a nut allergy. I don't mean a list of names as to who has an allergy. I mean a list of names and a picture of that child or maybe introducing them to the staff. Maybe different colored trays (if the individual doesn't want to stand out). Since some of our children are non verbal everyone should step up to ensure a safe environment. Needless to say that was the last time my daughter ever bought lunch at school. It has taken her years to be able to go out to a restaurant and know what to order and who to trust. If her environment had taken her safety first and was nurturing and educating my daughter would've had a much better experience and not trauma attached to this life threatening allergy. The only thing I came up with to remedy this was to buy her a medical bracelet and tell her if she is having an anaphylactic shock to tell her friends to stand on the table and scream to get the cafeteria staff to notice. Obviously, she never had to since I packed her lunch every day since then. Thank God.

It would be great if the Red Cross would come up with a signal for anaphylactic shock. There are several more allergies as well. We need to be proactive not reactive. This goes for the classrooms as well. If a child has a nut allergy it should fall on the teacher to remind parents to not bring in the allergen food into the classroom, as well as no surprise treats, etc. I did remedy this by always giving a box of treats that my daughter could have when a treat was brought into the classroom until a teacher decided the treat my daughter had was too big compared to the treat handed out and the teacher decided to not give my daughter anything. Yep the whole class got a treat but not my daughter! My hope is in this community schools districts hire individuals that have compassion, understanding, treat every child fairly and have training. Classrooms should be quieter with tennis balls on the chairs, there should be noise limitations. When a child covers their ears they are physically in pain. It's not just loud. They are trying to stop the noise from entering inorder to stop being in pain. We/Teachers/Aides need to acknowledge this and ask the class to be quieter. If the student can wear headphones that is great, but it's not realistic to ask them to wear them all day. You have to ask yourself "Would you want to wear headphones all day?" He refuses airpods, air plugs, and headbands as well. Making this an extremely difficult situation. He has no choice but to wear them when we go into public places. Smaller class sizes would also help with the noise level.

Classrooms with video surveillance like daycares would also help parents. The Bell and announcements! Wow, kind of explanatory I think. I understand a bell has to be in classrooms but it doesn't have to be on volume 10. Same with announcements. Everyone who is in school can hear the announcements. They shouldn't be so loud that the parking lot can hear them, as well as not being all throughout the day, maybe only 2x's a day and at the same time, so we can prepare the kids. Locked doors, double doors should be a must so elopers can't get out and of course, so no one can get in.

There should be non-standardized tests for non verbal children/adults. How can you give a nonverbal child/adult a test that is for typical children who can't talk? Schools and colleges should mimic this as well. They should have activities and classes to offer more support to everyone. In this community, the sidewalks would be large enough for golf carts, bikers, and walkers. I think having an autopilot golf cart trolley system would create so much independence upon the older generation who wishes to drive around the community, but cannot. The system would take them to a destination giving confidence and independence and ensure their safety. There should be cameras and Aids, if needed, on these golf carts as well. I also believe there should be pools in the subdivisions, and a couple of them. People are extremely loud in pools including my son. With a couple of pools in each subdivision it will give an opportunity for the individuals that have social anxiety and SPD a choice to pick between which pool to go to. Wheelchair lifts should be at every pool as well. Aquatic therapy and swim lessons should be offered weekly. Indoor pools should also be throughout the community. Ocean and water are the number one calming modalities for most of us, let alone with special needs. The indoor pools need to somehow not be so echoey. I'm challenging someone to figure out a way to stop that echo. I also think multiple different levels of books should be in classrooms and that an adult should not only read children's books. My son needs to read age-appropriate books, not children's books. Yes like all of us we have our favorite books but from an educational standpoint they need to be read books of all different genres. So let's give them the knowledge they crave!

Motivative programs should be incorporated as well. For example, if my son had good behavior for the week he could ride on the golf cart on Fridays. This was highly motivating to reduce his behavior until I found out the reason behind his behavior. Whatever works to motivate your child should be considered as long as it's safe. Making the child/adult feel independent is huge for my son. He wanted to be left alone for a while, not having an aide close to him, as well as he wanted to walk down the hallway by himself (with staff watching) to the vending machine. I had to pay for an advocate and fought for six months to get my son switched to another school and it made a world of difference. His teacher and aid were absolutely amazing and flexible. They allowed me to come to school whenever I wanted and worked with me and my son. My hope is in this community our schools have amazing individuals like these two men. Yes I said men. We need more men to be in the classrooms. My son is surrounded by women all day and evening. It is wonderful that he now has men in his life at school. Yes women bring a lot to the table please don't get me wrong but I fully believe boys need male role models in their life. I also believe there should be a Big Brother program for our children/adults. Bless my son's heart. He is so lonely and sad daily that he doesn't have a friend. It breaks my heart. He gets depressed a lot saying mom you don't understand. As much as we need to get our time, I believe our child needs to have their time with a friend, at least once a week. This is challenging for my son due to him being nonverbal, but when he was 5 years old he had a sweet little boy in his class whom they became best friends for one fun year and that child was verbal. That child went on to mainstream typical schools and they lost each other, but his mom and I still keep in contact. Since then my son hasn't had a friend, no matter how hard we have tried. Unfortunately he is extremely lonely and depressed, and it breaks my heart. Let's try to help our children whether they are verbal or not, in wheelchairs or not, by having a wonderful program where friends and family can get together and celebrate.

My last thought of schools is that I believe they should be year round. The first way is the same way that some schools currently run typical schools, except during the summer time they would have a two week break at the end of school, go back to school for four weeks, which is really like a camp no academics, because for most of our children they need consistency, and then at the end of the four weeks they would have another two weeks off before going back into school in the fall. Hopefully there shouldn't be much regression with only a two week break. The second way would be like some schools run. Typically, they would go to school for a couple of months and then have off for two weeks. Go to school for a couple of months and have off for two weeks. This rotation would be year-round. When children have off there should be camps set up for those parent/s who work full time. These camps should provide aids to children who need aids, not make the parents find an aid then pay for the aid and for the week of camp. This defeats the purpose on many levels.

5

Siblings

I think siblings tend to feel that they get lost in special-needs families. I think because of physical limitations, financial constrictions, and medical requirements, siblings are forced to grow up too fast. I know for myself, my daughter had to grow up way too fast due to autism, divorce, and her own life treating tree nut allergy. I never wanted her to feel like she was left out or have animosity towards her brother. I would single parent her as well as parent my son, which is like five boys in one. If I wanted to take them to a movie I would take my daughter to the movie the weekend before taking both of them to the same movie at the theatre for the sensory film day. This way she wouldn't miss out on seeing the movie just because we had to leave early, even during the sensory film. If some of you don't know what sensory film day, it's when you go to the theatre for a movie with lights on but dimmed, no previews, the volume is turned down drastically, you can bring your own food, the tickets are half-price, and you don't have to sit still while being quiet. If your child needs to move up and down the isles and can. This movie day is usually on a Saturday morning for one showing once a month. I feel there has to be a program where siblings can enjoy hanging out and be part of a group where someone else won't judge them and/or is in the same situation. We've always and still are making accommodations for my son no matter what we do, like if we take a 2 day vacation a year. It is extremely difficult for my daughter at times.

For the first time in her life she has met another person who has a special brother who is nonverbal and uses a keyboard to communicate. It shouldn't have taken her 18 years to find someone like this. These programs need to be put into place as well as, outdoor activities, and sports, etc. It will be a place of sanctuary and fun with absolutely no bullying and no judgement. I truly believe our children will be such understanding, compassionate, passionate young adults. What our world needs today. No negativity, only encouragement for everyone else. This same camaraderie should be carried through in schools and in college. No bullying policies, classes on how to cope, sports and activities where everyone works together. Some events with their siblings and others without. Unity and individuality is needed to show that "I can still shine on my own" and "I can hang with my siblings and have fun" or "not feel guilty" because they don't want to hang with their special needs siblings.

A side note for parents, siblings, family members, I think there should be an 800 help/support line 24/7 set into place and serve as a support group to meet different times, places etc for all of us. I don't think it should fall to parents to set this up. There should always be support and help for us as individuals and/or family. Meetings/groups can be for siblings for Information to learn what to do in difficult situations as well different modalities, and having fun getting together, etc. I had my daughter take a couple of day classes on this when she was young. I myself have always taken day courses on diet, vitamins, sensory modalities, etc. Anything to educate myself and make our situation easier. These courses were very helpful for us and I recommend everyone take them as well.

6

Must haves in this community

I believe there should be a community watch program in place, especially for elopers, some kind of tracking device that isn't invasive or impinging on their rights and possibly gated communities so no one gets lost. I know this is a hot topic but it needs to have a solution. We can't have our children getting lost no matter what. I know there are a lot of devices and trinkets out there, but for my son he is unable to use most of them due to his sensory processing disorder. If you have any suggestions please let me know.

I think Special Olympics should be offered several times a year, as well as league games. I believe all police personnel and first responders should be trained to know what behaviors look like, as well as the modalities used to rectify a situation. They shouldn't just charge and assume that person is on drugs. There are adaptive items you can buy for your car like stickers and seat belt covers, which help, but they may not be noticeable when personnel enter the scene. Police officers need to know how to respond to a nonverbal person or that a person may act out when being touched or in stressful situations. There needs to be some kind of system where first responders know the house they are entering has a special needs person and what they need to do to take the safety precautions. In case of a fire my child would just sit there and not respond to someone else entering the house. The fire department/first responders needs to know whether a person is nonverbal. When taking vitals this information would be crucial. Just like police officers and first responders are trained on Diabetes, seizures, drunk individuals, they should also know about special needs. I know of a mother whose child had a high tolerance of pain and got into an accident while driving and the first responders didn't take him to the hospital because he said he wasn't in pain. Yet when his parents arrived on the scene and told him to go to the hospital, the doctors said he had broken his neck. These scary situations need to be prevented with training.

Music therapy is a must in this community. All individuals reep wonderful benefits with music. Let's help our children/adults to enjoy it more by learning how to play or just listen to the instruments. Gatherings of parents who know how to play instruments and want to share and teach our kids.

We need to have special needs attorneys to be able to help us understand our rights and help us with guardianship, power of attorney, and much more. Just as important are financial consultants to help us and our children for the future, Able accounts, 401(k), etc. The individual consultant I have for my financial needs is very knowledgeable and specializes in special needs accounts. If you need to get a financial consultant I would highly recommend him. His information is in the Resources chapter. I think working a part-time job or a remote would be the best situation for most individuals, as well as planning for the future, and budgeting, and he can help you with that, if you wish. Even if you think you have nothing to save, he will find a way to help you.

Of course there should be bowling alleys, sports arenas, golf courses, racquetball, etc. in this community. The men in our lives need to relieve stress as well. And for those women who love these activities all the power to ya! Having outings and events for everyone should be monthly, if not weekly. Dancing, rides, Petting zoos, tractor rides, concerts, are all wonderful social events. It would be great if someone could figure out how to get a ball to return to you in a tennis court and a basketball court, another challenge for someone. Walking trails/sidewalks should be wheelchair accessible including being labelled, as well as horseback riding. I think parks should have trampolines at the ground level so no one gets hurt. My son would jump on his trampoline for two hours a day. I believe this community should have farm programs for veggie growing and how to take care of animals, cleaning, brushing and feeding them. Being outdoors with animals and digging in the dirt is so beneficial on multiple levels. Of course pet therapy is a must as well. Once or two times weekly pet therapy animals should come into school or day programs or assisted living housing. I grew up on a farm and had several family members in the farming industry. I have the utmost respect for their hard work and the food they provide for us.

For myself, having my own horse was truly a gift. We also had pigs, chickens, turkey, and a beef cow that we butchered ourselves. To this day, we all still laugh about our childhood and cringe, LOL. Let me tell you how beneficial that was for all of us to live so healthy. My parents to this day still have their garden after 40 years, and they still can live off of the fat of the land. My dad runs his husky dogs on a sled, and my mom still has her horses and chickens. They do all of this with only 5 acres. My cousin will give them deer, bear, and salmon for their freezer. My uncle has amazing hay for their horses, and my other uncle has the best tasting corn on the cob and beef cow. My parents are extremely healthy individuals and my hat goes off to them for being able to live like that still to this day.

Hair salons should have devices that have minimal noise to cut hair. Maybe a TV or iPad for distractions and a good cape to ensure all the hair is collected and not on the child or adult. A hair dresser that isn't loud and is very conscious about what she's doing. When some autisic children get a haircut they say it actually hurts them. Telling a child/adult to just put up with it or that they don't know what they are talking about is degrading. It's just like noise actually hurts them. It's not just loud, it actually hurts them. Our children have special needs and we have to adjust what we do to help them to not be in pain.

Airplane simulators would be a must in this community. One that gives the accurate pressure of turbulence, ascending and descending, in order to help individuals understand what it is really like on a plane. On real planes they have to make the seats larger, have more legroom, and the announcements quieter. A program to simulate going through the airport and the security system is also crucial as well.

I think when building the roads of this community there should be enough room on the shoulder for us to pull over for an emergency like for bathroom accidents, vomiting and meltdowns, Etc.

My thoughts on cameras in the community are yes, yes, yes! Cameras should be on buses and in schools, daycare, and public businesses. Tyler has been physically abused several times in his life. Each situation we were told that we cannot use devices to record anything. The cops, CPS, judges, law guardians, and therapists all did not believe my children. Mainly because my son is nonverbal. During one of these events when the cops looked at my son's bruises and they said that they had seen worse, that they aren't a proactive system, only reactive. My children still deal with these traumas today. Not something children should have to go through just because they are nonverbal. If there were cameras allowed I believe these things would have stopped, at least there would've been proof of these events.

The other thing I have no tolerance for is the "R" Word. If it is used correctly in a sentence as mental tardation, that's one thing but using it in a derogatory statement is the same as calling an African-American the "N" word. It is not needed and I'm not sure why it's still so acceptable. With all of these changes going on in the world regarding race, why isn't this in the forefront too? We need to make sure we have amazing people with higher standards, compassion, empathy, just like one of my son's prior teachers and one of his prior pediatricians. They are amazing individuals who always made my son feel loved and respected. A pediatrician that actually believed me when it came to my son. Kudos to these individuals. Please keep doing what you're doing, you are amazing.

HealthCare needs to have much lower deductibles and payments monthly for special needs families, single parents, etc. There needs to be a shift in the states payment scale for Respite workers, daycare workers, geratic centres. We don't need workers abusing our children/adults because they don't get paid. This issue has been going on for a long time and I know it's not an easy one to change, maybe in our community we can figure out a way to make this possible.

Child Support is another issue that needs to be addressed. I filed to relocate to South Carolina because my son's care aid, my twin, moved. She had moved in with us when I filed for divorce and took on the parent role for my children. She would go with us to doctors, hospital visits, etc. She has been there for us in every way possible. When she moved I had no one to help me. Moving out of state, even though my son is severely disabled, meant losing child support. I had to make a decision to relocate. Special needs costs never end therefore, the parent paying child support should always have to pay until 21 years of age. There should be stricter laws protecting the parent who cares for the child. The other parent doesn't take on any of the responsibilities of the parent who the child lives with. I know there are a lot of women out there who never see their ex or don't get help physically, so let's not take away the father's financial responsibility to pay child support.

Let's talk about Halloween and golf carts. My son loves his golf cart (given to us as a gift from our sweet hearted cousin), but especially on Halloween. My son is able to go to multiple houses because he cannot walk a lot. His knees have developed half their size and they both sit laterally. They have both dislocated two times each. He will have to have surgery to move the kneecap where it should be and then attach a ligament to his chin bone and his kneecap in order to keep the knee in the correct position. We cannot do surgery until my son has finished growing. So unfortunately, this creates a huge obstacle because of his sensory processing disorder. We cannot use a trampoline, the pool, the beach, anything that we have used in the past 15 years. He is extremely guarded that it will dislocate again. Therefore, I still have to put his shoes on for him which we both know he does not like. If we do the surgery before he is done growing and he grows more than an inch after the surgery, the ligament will stretch and break/rip apart. So it is a waiting game for now, and the golf cart really helps us. We used it for motivation as well. I believe it is ridiculous for people to make a child say trick-or-treat in order to receive a bite size candy especially when they are nonverbal, and have anxiety, etc. The blue pumpkin is a great idea, but I don't think people understand what it means. It's a simple, perfect, system and people don't know what it is for. No one should expect a child/adult to say "treat or treat" if they are holding this blue pumpkin.

Churches need private rooms, just in case they are needed, that have break proof windows so you can still watch the sermon. Speaker volume should be turned down and let elopers and people with anxiety out the door first. Please don't make them wait. More services offered so the church isn't packed, as well as limiting the amount of people going to service.

I believe houses should be ranches with the bedrooms down the hall and away from the kitchen and living room, for noise reduction. Duplexes are also good, but I would like these homes being built with noise reducing products to be sprayed in between the walls to ensure quietness. I believe the bathrooms should be large enough for two adults to not hit the sink or toilet. I would like to see showers made with built-in hand rails and seats. Some kind of waterproof pecs board so if an individual needs picture instruction to take a shower it's there for them. Also some kind of hot and cold identifiers on the faucets. For example, I put painter's tape on the shower wall and the knob so when my son turns on the water he knows to match the two pieces of tape to get warm water. Of course the fans would have to be quieter. I'm not sure how that would work but I'm sure someone could come up with a solution. We are not able to put the fan on ever, which of course leads to mold. If you have any suggestions I would love to hear them.

7

The future

I believe the programs should be educational not just work programs. They should teach ADLs (activities of daily living), cooking, cleaning, money management, and have community outings. Residential programs should have houses that have four bedrooms, not five or more. Staffing twenty four hours seven days a week is a must for nonverbal individuals but not 24 hours shifts like I used to do. There should be assisted living apartments where staff is at the office 9 to 5 Monday through Friday in case of an emergency or just to help, otherwise these individuals can live pretty independently.

There should also be enough houses to support the number of individuals. There are no group homes available now. And let's be honest, ten years ago the waitlist was 10 years. I was told to get my son on that waiting list ASAP. The fact that parents have to take out a second mortgage with 2 to 3 other parents who have to have children in a home setting, is absolutely unthinkable. Once again, it's up to the parents to take care of the children and it should not be. Of course this doesn't include the 3 to 4 parents sharing the cost of aides and their responsibility to take care of each individual. It's infuriating to think about. I know several parents would never put a child/adult in a group home setting and that is ok. That is their choice, but for those of us who think it's acceptable, we need to have a better plan for now, not just in the future. I've been in the health field for 30+ years as a home health aide, working in group homes with mentally ill and developmentally disabled individuals, occupational therapy assistant, dental assistant, and assistant in an embryology lab. I've seen firsthand how things haven't gotten better. How the responsibility is still on the parent, even after all these years. Who will take care of our children after we're gone? It's an extremely difficult situation to talk about considering our children live to be 80 and 90 years old. Well I think it's time to start talking and just start making changes for a better world for our families. I don't want my son going to the state or having my daughter take care of him after I am no longer here.

We need to have support groups to socialize in the form of Meet ups to pinpoint your specific interest. Educational seminars to educate family, friends, professionals, law enforcements etc. You can also create your own group or sponsor a group with your time and knowledge. With social media, it should be much easier to get the word out about groups or meetings or events. We do need several companies and family members to help us with this. Whether your support group comes from the family, friends, social networking, social events, athletic events, seminars, outings for parents, etc. they are a must. We need more support groups offered more frequently. I'm calling on you to help make this happen.

We need to get back to canning, being outdoors, turning off electronics, no microwaves, no fake lighting or LED lights, no long hours at work, etc. This is all possible. Now is the time to make serious changes and stand up for our beliefs. Several studies show that we are more productive in a 6 hour workday than an 8-10 hour workday. Mentally, We don't work past six hours, our brains just can't do that. So we use the other two hours to take lunch, smoke breaks, and talk with coworkers. I'm sure you agree that spending time with your family and getting more sleep as well as getting more time at home is much more important than those extra two hours during the day at work. We need to simplify the way we live.

Having longer maternity leave as well as leave for fathers. More time off a year in general, more time to do these things leads to more quality work, quality family life, and employees who come to work on time and have less sick days because they aren't sick that often. Using holistic care to take care of ourselves I find, is extremely crucial. Using Eastern medicine in our daily lives yet reaping the benefits of Western medicine when we need it. In the past 15 years I have spent $150,000 and two bankruptcies trying to remove toxins from my son and helping him so that his body could be stronger, fight off infections, and not be bombarded with chemicals. It's just throwing money out the door. Shame on the companies who charge us an arm and leg because they put the word "autism" on something and charge more money. We already struggle with medical bills. Let's work together in this community to make sure this doesn't happen. I have seen amazing things from Western medicine and I believe we need it but not in our daily lives. We can use remedies, herbs, organic food, etc. in our daily lives and to heal many illnesses. In the following chapter I list all of the modalities I've tried on my son to help his body remove toxins and build his immune system. I know there are a ton more modalities out there, and I feel we need these options out there for us to choose and give us control and power as to what we feel will help/benefit our children and ourselves.

Time for the vaccine talk. If you want to skip this section please jump to the next chapter. I feel it is up to the parents as to when and how many vaccines your child should get. Therefore, in this community there will be no vaccine demand. I am a firm believer that my son's disability was from a set of circumstances including but not limited to vaccines. My son had 100% lead, mercury, titanium, aluminium, and arsenic in his little body by the time he was 18 months old. Being coerced into taking the flu shot while six months pregnant from the nurse and the doctor was very damaging. At the six-month appointment I was told four times, two times by each, that I would kill my son if I did not get the flu shot. Not knowing just how damaging my stressful marriage was on my unborn child, giving him a low immune system, his pre-birth plan, the additional toxins from baby formula, food, the environment, his childhood trauma, as well as the vaccines which led up to his autism. Which is why already in his weakened state his body and soul we're giving up letting the vaccines harm him instead of building antibodies.

Lets not forget about the medicines the doctor prescribed him, and general anesthesia at 15 months of age for his first set of ear tubes. My son has had 4 sets of ear tubes, 4 ruptured eardrums, and over 17 ear infections from nine months of age until now. His last ruptured eardrum happened in 2018 and it has not healed. The ENT wants us to do a surgery which will take 2 1/2 hours to take a skin graft from the back of his ear to heal the hole inside his ear. Whether you want to give your child a vaccine or not is your choice, not the state's, governments or pharmaceutical companies. There are plenty of doctors with different vaccine schedules for your child, spacing them out and getting the most important ones first, for example Dr. Sears[1]. Maybe waiting a year after birth to let our children's body develop and grow should be the first step. Either decision you make is your decision not the medical field's decision. And I know you're going to say that we have to have shots in order to get our children into daycare. I say, then now is the time in this community to help each other out. If you feel you want to wait a year, that should be your choice. A child should not be ostracized for not getting shots.

Several countries let the mom stay home for the most crucial year of their child's life, why don't we? For example, the hepatitis shot says right on the label do not administer to anyone under the age of 18 years old. So this begs the question: why give this vaccine to the child the first day they are born? Your liver is not 100% functioning until you're six months of age. If you want this vaccine, wait until you're 18 years old like the instructions say. Splitting the MMR is beneficial, you can have your child's titers tested to see if his or her body has developed its own antibodies for that specific disease that you are testing. Don't just take or give these toxic filled vaccines before doing research. The bonus program that doctors get for giving your child a vaccine should be burned and unfortunately, pharmaceutical companies are too powerful, so yes, doctors get paid when they give your child a vaccine. So maybe as a society/community we should not be shamed or be coerced as to whether we should give our child a vaccine. There are several options to take, not just get vaccinated.

Haven't we learned from Covid? We were all told that the Covid vaccine would stop the spread of the disease and in fact the majority of individuals who had the Covid vaccine got

---

[1] Dr Sears Alternative vaccine Schedule. Web site is in the Resources Chapter

Covid. Isn't that the point of a vaccine is to stop the disease from spreading, but it did not. Yet there is no talk of that, is there. It was, all take the vaccine, take the vaccine, now there's no talking at all. In history all diseases take their course usually lasting one and a half to two years and then they die off. If we had a strong immune system to begin with these diseases wouldn't last very long. The vaccines were usually introduced by the time that disease was in an endemic state, which means it was already starting to die off therefore, the vaccine had no benefit. There are several documentations out there to prove this.

Diseases will unfortunately always be there, so we need to rely on ourselves to be healthier for when these illnesses happen. We shouldn't keep bombarding our bodies, we should eat healthy, organically, no industrialized farming, no GMO, and stop putting all these toxins in our body and environment. We have the power to change this. We are the consumer. What we buy will get sold. We can build a community where farmers can farm lands organically and processed foods should go bye-bye. We need to start somewhere. Look, the government and pharmaceutical companies aren't going to change the vaccine schedule because if they reduce the amount of vaccines given to our children, our children stop getting so sick, and no one would believe the doctors anymore. So let's stop fighting them. Let's take control of what we do and how we vaccinate our children. No shaming, and no bullying, just helping each other out. All of these toxins from everywhere are making us sick: Alzheimer's, dementia, cancer, nut allergies, anxiety, mental illness, and depression, the list goes on. We are well aware that these numbers have been on the rise for the past decade, let's start taking responsibility for what we are doing. My goal is to live as long as I possibly can so I can help my son, and not to die a horrible early death to leave him without a mother.

8
Modalities

Modality is the way or mode in which something exists or is done. Here is a list of modalities I have used in the past 17 years. Like I said before, there are so many modalities out there to try. Here are a few that have dramatically helped my son heal. Many of these modalities you will know about. My wish is that you will try one of these or several of these to find which one works for you and your family. I am choosing to not go into detail about these modalities. I just wanna give you a brief description of them, and how they did or didn't help us. The contact info and websites for you to research are in the "Resources" chapter. My disclaimer is I am not a doctor, just a consumer who has tried what I felt would've been beneficial to my son. Please use these modalities with your own discretion. Please don't do anything that you don't think will help your family.

1) **Energy testing/muscle testing**. Energy testing is a way of asking your body if what I'm doing or putting in my body has a positive or negative impact

energetically. You can use your fingers, your body, and or a pendulum. We use this in our daily lives and have been for the past 10 years. It is the most beneficial tool we use. Connecting with our energy and keeping ourselves healthy through energy healing will change your life.

2) **Muscle testing**. Muscle testing is the same concept as energy testing but it uses your muscles to test and diagnose elements by applying slight pressure to parts of your body. Chiropractors and physical therapists, as well as occupational therapists use this methodology in their practice. We use this in our daily lives as well and have been for the past 10 years. Both of these, energy and muscle testing have helped us to get clarity and to have the power as to what is in my family's highest interest and benefit. If I don't have my pendulum with me for an energy test I will muscle test. For example in the store If I'm not sure I should buy a certain vitamin I muscle test for it. I will hold the object to my stomach and ask if it's in my highest and best interest to eat this/ take this. If my body sways forward that means "yes" and if it sways backwards it's a "no". This gives me the complete control to know if I should have this product.

3) **Energy Psychologist/Healers**. Healers help individuals in many ways by utilizing multiple modalities to help clear trauma and negative beliefs. Our healer has been my family's healer for the last two years. She uses several of these modalities listed as well as gives you a different perspective on a situation. She also has made me accountable for myself, being aware as to when I get upset, how to calm myself down, and helping my children as well as self-care with Flower essence,

recommending doctors in the area, giving me homework to do for the week as well as working on fertility (for other individuals), biomagnetic therapy, and much much more. If you don't have a healer, I highly recommend one. I can't thank our healer enough for introducing me to most of these modalities. For always being flexible and wanting to make flower essence last minute, teaching me these modalities so I am informed and have the power to make decisions for my family indefinitely. We thank our healer for everything she has done for us. If you wish to contact her I have put her information in the Resources chapter.

4) **Life Coach**. Life coaches are always extremely helpful. They counsel you on your career and any personal challenge you may have. I found our healer, so I did not pursue a life coach, but I met an amazing life coach after I was working with our healer. Life coaches take a slightly different approach but are just as important as healers. Their experiences and knowledge are equally as valuable as healers. They have you complete exercises to help you look at yourself and your life to make the changes you want to see.

5) **Biomagnetism**. Biomagnetic therapy is a non-invasive approach using a pair of magnets to create an electromagnetic field through your body in order to restore relaxation, reduce inflammation, stop infections, heal bones and scar tissue, control pain, support balance and well-being. When you have a session with biomagnets you won't believe how relaxed you are afterwards as well as how calm you feel. I have been doing biomagnetics therapy with this healter for the last two years and highly recommend it. When my son's gut

or ears hurt him he will ask for magnets. Magnets and TAT (see below) are the only two modalities that he asks for daily. The magnets reduce his pain within half an hour and he is able to function for the day.

6) **Emotional Freedom Technique (EFT)/ TAPPING.** EFT is used for physical pain in emotional distress. Tapping is a form of acupuncture to balance your energy system and to reduce anxiety, stress, PTSD and depression. I have taught this to my children to use as a tool in their daily lives. There are several exercises to choose from. You can tap or press on a point of the body to achieve the same effect. Donna Eden[2] uses her own tapping techniques as well. My daughter will use the technique of pushing instead of tapping on her upper lip to relax herself when she is anxious and feels like passing out. For example, when drawing blood she had passed out before and now using this tapping/ holding technique she doesn't pass out. When she needs to feel confident she will press her fingers on her chin acting like she's thinking but in reality she's holding a pressure point to help her feel confident. Tapping on your thymus (between your chest on your chest bone) for 30-60 seconds will wake you up and help you focus again. These simple techniques are very effective, quick and easy.

7) **Occupational Therapy**. OT can help people in several ways with any age who have cognitive, physical, or sensory processing disorder. My son has been on a sensory diet for years. Since I graduated as an occupational therapy assistant many, many moons ago, adapting and modifying to situations has come

---

[2] www.edenmethod.com

natural to me. When my son was young I turned my rec/bonus room into a sensory haven for him with a swing, (yep I had a swing in my house), a rocking horse, a bolster, a mini trampoline, and lots of sensory toys, ball pit and several different shaped and textured balls. I would conduct OT exercises on him daily to calm his nervous system. As well as I would use the Wilbarger therapy brush before going on an outing. This is a brush you would use on your child and then conduct joint compression activities to calm his nervous system. It's a quick, easy, and cheap way to help your child out. You can get this brush online but I recommend a OT help you with instructions to make sure you are doing it correctly. I would also have ball pits in my house. I would use a kiddie pool and fill the plastic balls in the pool and have my son roll and jump in it. I would use the therapy ball to roll on my son to relax his nerves as well as have him bounce on it to wake him up. Yes my son has hyper and hypo sensory processing disorder. Meaning at times he seeks the environment to wake him up and other times he needs to get away or use equipment to help him relax. The speech therapist and I would work together as I would bounce my son on the therapy ball or when he was on the trampoline we would sing the alphabet to introduce and reiterate the alphabet Because with movement he was and is always able to hear. When we had him sit in front of us making eye contact his auditory senses would shut down.

8) **Physical Therapist.** PT helps injury, deformity, and treatment of disease using muscle testing, heat treatment, cupping, tens unit, and exercise instead of surgery or drugs. On a side note, physical therapy

for my son was never approved through a school evaluation, even though he has been toe walking since he was two years of age, because there was no bathing or stairs needed at school. Therefore, if you want PT, you will have to pay privately to help out with toe walking and other physical needs that you may have with your child. Of course this was 6 to 10 years ago and I tried to get this covered. It may be a different story now.

9) **Cupping**. Cupping is when a therapist puts special cups on your skin to create a suction to bring the blood to a stagnant area of your body, as well as reduce pain inflammation and promote relaxation. You may have seen Olympic athletes with circles "hickeys" on them, this is cupping. My son used this during his physical therapy sessions after his dislocations for his knees. They would put the cups on his thighs (adductor) muscles to relax them from being so tight and to stop pulling his knee out of socket. I continue to use this in my daily life for my shoulder and back pain as well. I will also use it on my son for his neck and back pain.

10) **SomaticTherapy**. Somatic therapy helps with PTSD and other mental health conditions using stretching, Reiki, Energy and muscle testing to connect a person's mind and body. Our somatic therapist is amazing, she focuses on stimulating my son's Vagus nerve to stop any of his ear and head pain, as well as stretching, Reiki, and other modalities. She is extremely passionate, compassionate, and knowledgeable. She is always willing to adapt to my sons' pain and she is helping me with my scar tissue and extreme back pain. She works

with all ages. I have her contact information in the Resources chapter.

11) **Reiki**. Reiki is an energy healing technique that reduces stress and anxiety and promotes relaxation through gentle touch or no touch at all. My son really feels the wonderful effects of Reiki when our somatic therapist works with him. In fact, he will ask for it for any gut, ear, or knee pain that he has. She will also help him align his chakras, giving him an exercise to practice on his own to also help align his chakras.

12) **Tomatis Method**. Tomatis method is a sound therapy to improve sensory issues, improve listening, and communication skills. A person uses headphones to listen to music, usually Mozart, and other sounds. My son did this therapy in New York and it did help his sensory processing disorder a little bit. He would go into the school where it was conducted and put headphones on while listening to mozart. I believe this was daily for one month. After which he was able to have me wipe him down with a towel after a shower or wipe his hands when they were dirty.

13) **Cranial Sacral Therapy**. CST is a light touch to examine membranes and movement of fluids in and around the central nervous system, and release tension in the nervous system. Occupational therapists and chiropractors use this modality. We have used cranial sacral therapy in the past with both a chiropractor and an occupational therapy assistant. With the chiropractor she would slowly hold his ears, activating the vagus nerve as well as rubbing downward from his ears to his clavicle. She would work very slowly on his head releasing tension and to get the blood flowing. We

conducted this therapy for a year in conjunction with a homeopathic doctor.

14) **Homeopathic Doctors**. Homeopathic doctors heal the whole body, not symptom/s. They use "like cures like" with remedies, meaning a symptom of a disease in a healthy person that can cure similar symptoms in a sick person. They promote organic healthy eating and many more clean living modalities. I started using a homeopathic doctor when my son was 4 years old. This amazing doctor told us to eat green leafy vegetables, suggested a Gluten Free diet, and gave us some remedies. After a week of doing what she asked, my son had no more diarrhea, an issue he had since birth. This launched me into the homeopathic world forever.

15) **Gluten free casein free diet/parasite cleanse**. A GFCF diet is very helpful. Yes it is a challenge to stay on or stick to it but it is extremely beneficial with gut health, memory clarity, and less tantrums. Once you incorporate this diet it becomes second nature. Staying away from dyes, natural flavoring, additives, sugar, and antibiotics will also help your child to not have extreme highs and lows. Parasite cleansing once a month will also help these issues you may have. After our visit with our homoeopathic doctor I started making lots of stews, soups, and marinara made with lots of green veggies. With my son's SPD it is a challenge to try new things constantly and we tried and tried for years. He has been eating mashed potatoes because I added cauliflower to change the thick consistency of normal potatoes. Last year was the first year he didn't gag with the smell of eggs and now eats scrambled eggs, but not any other

eggs. This is the same with sweet potatoes. He will eat them if they are baked in a goodie or in the air fryer as french fries, but not mashed. I haven't found a good veggie to add to sweet potatoes that will change the taste. Anyway, what I'm saying is keep trying. I know how hard it is that your child/adult eats chicken nuggets and macaroni and cheese, but consistency will prevail. There are so many cookbooks, YouTube, TickTock's, and Pinterest, that show you different ways to make food. Of course, probiotics and liver detox are essential for helping you and your child get rid of toxins and to have a healthy gut. Many people believe in parasite cleansing monthly to improve their intestines and illuminate parasites from the body without using prescription medications. This helps with heart health, skin health, weight management, mental health, and improved digestion. We have tried this in the past and will be doing this again in the near future.

16) **Applied Behavioral Analysis**. Applied behavioral analysis/ABA is interpersonal therapy in which a child works one on one with an ABA practitioner. ABA practitioners use this modality with daily living skills and speech. My son did ABA 15 hours a week along with speech therapy daily and occupational therapy 5 times a week. At the age of two he had a "work" week of 20 plus hours a week, He did ABA until he was five years old. His experience wasn't a pleasant one but I know ABA has helped out other individuals. It all depends on your child. My son's ABA teacher was amazing with him. I am still friends with her to this day. She loves her job, loves working with children, helped my son with food issues, and has helped many, many children.

We love her so much. She puts everything she has into that job to help special needs children. My child went to a private school after the age of five and it was an amazing school. He had some truly amazing teachers at this school. I wish for these caring individuals in this community.

17) **Letter Board Communication**. There are a couple of forms of letter board/keyboard communication. I started my son on this form of communication several years ago. The woman who created this for her son has helped thousands of individuals learn how to communicate by pointing, writing or typing.[3] This program has helped my son tenfold. My son types on a keyboard to communicate with me daily. Although my son is still sad about being nonverbal, at least he has a way to tell us his needs, thoughts, and what hurts him. This program worked for my son because he did not need to make eye contact, and he could still complete sensory tasks to stay focused as the session was in progress. I knew my son was inside there somewhere, I just needed to find the right program for him. I urge you to not give up. There is some type of modality that will work for your child. Many of my son's behaviors stopped because he could now communicate at school and at home. Although some individuals have been "Cured" from Autism this was never my intent. I don't think Autism is a bad thing. In fact, I think it is a gift. I have tried these modalities to reduce or stop my son's physical and mental pain and not to cure him.

18) **BioMedical Treatment**. Biomedical treatment uses the hyperbaric chamber, special diet, hair testing,

---

[3] See Resource chapter for her website

chelation, probiotics, and high-dose vitamins. I attempted to use all of these forms of treatment years ago with no avail. Years ago this treatment was called DAN "defeat autism now", but was discontinued in 2011. The chelation wouldn't work because my son's veins collapsed and therefore, no medicine could get in or out. This treatment uses transdermal medicine, B12 shots, supernuthera, as well as other vitamins and chelation. I am not saying they won't work for someone, I'm just saying they didn't work for my son. I still use other forms of biomedical treatment like probiotics and vitamins just not in the high potency I used to give him.

19) **Hyperbaric Oxygen Therapy.** HBOT is when you are in a chamber and pure 100% oxygen is pushed through your cells to speed up healing for stubborn wounds, infections, and replace cells in the brain. Many people use HBOT in the chambers at home or offices to help them with the after effects of a stroke as well as athletes to recover from their injuries. We did attempt to try this but due to claustrophobia it got the better of us and we couldn't go through with it.

20) **Meditation/Yoga/Grounding/Earthing**. We all know about these techniques but if you don't, I would like to give you my thoughts. There are several forms of meditation. The form of meditation that works best for myself is Transcendental Meditation(TM). This meditation is for 10 minutes a day for children and 20 minutes a day for adults. You can't do this meditation before bed, it will keep you up. This type of meditation is meant to put you in a deeper state of relaxation than REM. It is meant for you to not stop your thoughts like some forms of yoga but to encourage the thoughts

to leave the mind so that you can revive and rejuvenate yourself. Some individuals do transcendental meditation two times daily, once in the morning and once in the evening. Morning is beneficial to get yourself relaxed and ready for the day and when you get back from work it helps you to destress from work and then you are more able to take on the next several hours in the evening. There are several famous individuals that use this technique to quiet the mind. I can't say enough great things about transcendental meditation. If you have a form of meditation and/or yoga you use, please stay with what works for you. Congrats keep up the great work. Special-needs parents have an extremely stressful environment, worrying about physical abuse, self injury, bullying, if school is going to call and say come pick your child up now and you have to leave work, etc. We need to find modalities that work for us and this is why I believe these zen gardens would be perfect in our community. We can use them at will while walking, while at work etc., but we need to build them. Grounding/Earthing uses your bare feet or grounding blankets to electronically reconnect you to earth so you reap the benefits mother nature gives you. We wear rubber shoes and walk on carpeted or wooden floors all day and/or concrete and asphalt, we are not in sunlight, etc. We need to get back to connecting with mother nature and feeling rejuvenated.

21) **Strategies in Crisis and Intervention and Prevention**. SCIP is for staff members with an approach of dealing with aggressive, violent, self-injury behavior during a "meltdown" crisis mode. I worked at group homes with mentally ill and developmentally

disabled for 10 years and we have to perform this move safely when needed. When my son was ten he became increasingly frustrated and aggressive so I had to start using SCIP on him at times (yes, I was crying the whole time). I did have a sensory room with a floor mat that I would lay on while I performed this. My son told me today (2022) that "we were not on the same page then mom". Due to his being nonverbal my son was aggressive, hitting the bus aide daily while going to school, hitting peers, and teachers, as well as my daughter and myself. He was extremely frustrated and he could not communicate what he needed. This is one time in our lives we don't like to look back on. I started administering Risperidone, because he was allergic to Prozac, and this allowed him to sleep for the first time in 10 years for at least seven hours straight a night. It also made him gain 50 pounds and we had to draw blood every six months. His aggressive behaviors pretty much ended, for a couple of years anyway. I no longer did SCIP moves on him and they removed the five point harness that they had to strap on him daily on the bus. That summer, I started teaching my son how to communicate on a leaderboard.

22) **Manifesting.** Manifesting is the practice of thinking a spiritual thought/thoughts with the intent of making them real. I use a manifesting technique called Theta waves manifestation where you can use your unconscious mind to take control to get what you desire. I also like to use a vision board before I go up into Theta. I try to manifest at least 3 to 5 times a week, but I would like to do it more. There are a lot of techniques to manifest, as well as several different quotes you can use to help

yourself daily. Before bed I usually ask the angels to remove the "collected" from the day or after existing certain buildings. I usually put a bubble around me or my vehicle before leaving the house or entering a building for protection against negative energy. You can envision a bubble, shield, or a screen where only the good can come in and the bad bounces off. I actually use this with people who stress me out or are negative. I want the good stuff to come in but not the bad stuff. Since I am an empath, I need to make sure I surround myself with protection, often. No matter what your shield/bubble is, it's your way of protecting yourself from negativity. When you leave a building or a room you can always rub your hands and swish your hands away from your body saying "anything that is collected needs to stay, It's not needed here". Another way of removing energy is to remove your clothing and change into something else, for example I removed my son's clothing after school because of all the chaos in class. It's a small thing you can do to ensure some of the "collected" has been removed.

23) **Transcranial Magnetic Stimulation**. TMS, not to be confused with electroconvulsive therapy/ECT, is a noninvasive form of brain stimulation in which a changing magnetic field is used to cause electric current at a specific area of the brain through electromagnetic induction. TMS will help the left and right hemispheres "talk" to each other again, as well as helping with depression, PTSD, and anxiety. You must be 18 years of age, as well as meet several other protocols that must be met in order to qualify for this treatment. We have been waiting one year already and will be starting this

treatment next May when my son turns 18. We are beyond excited for this therapy.

24) **Tapas Acupressure Technique.** TAT is a therapy that clears negative emotions and past traumas by using acupressure technique by holding points on your head and going through a series of statements. I have been working with my son on this technique for four months with the best results yet. In the next chapter I go into detail about just how this technique has changed our lives. It has also made my son and I even closer. We will continue to use this in our daily lives for other emotions we are having.

25) **Quantum K.** Quantum K meaning algorithm is a system that uses focused intent, fractal geometry, and harmonics to offer healing to the mind, body, and soul. My son and I have been working with an amazing healer from the UK this year and have made great strides in our life. We cannot thank him enough. He is an amazing healer and person. I also mention more about this healing in the next chapter, as well as his contact information is in the Resources chapter.

9

Bravery, healing from within

I feel I need to share a secret with you, but let me start by sharing with you my son's health issues over the last 6-8 months. My son started throwing up bile on a weekly basis in December of 2021. At first I thought it was from him gagging from a stuffy nose, that he was getting a cold, or that he ate something bad the night before. It took some time to rule out these possible outcomes. When you have a child/adult who is nonverbal you need to first rule out several things before making assumptions. First and foremost is the behavior from a sickness or from sensory processing disorder. If not, then I look at the environment and/or people in that environment. Once I find the root cause I can then attempt to help my son out. After sickness, allergy, and food were ruled out I found that the environment was good. What to do from this point? I switched to Eastern/Western medicine doctors/nurses six months prior so I asked them for help.

We conducted blood work, which in the past, my son could only do by going under general anaesthesia, but with this visit my son was able to sit at a lab and get blood drawn. Of course this came with a very slow trickle of blood taking 10 mins to get 1.5 vials and pricking him in another place to see if we could get more. He almost passed out and we had to have him sit and stay there for 10 extra minutes. This made the other patients mad because they had to wait longer. One person came into the exam area asking the nurse if she knew they were out there. My son had to hang onto my shoulders, hoping he wouldn't fall, while walking out to the van. This wonderful experience has made it even more difficult for him to want to draw blood again. His results came back stating nothing was wrong.

A week goes by and we are at my son's Somatic therapy appointment and he states it feels like his stomach is going to explode! He requested to go to the hospital knowing that he'd have to draw blood again and possibly have other tests completed. He did have to have blood drawn and again it showed nothing was wrong. He wanted his pain to go away so bad that he agreed to have a CT while at the hospital. First time ever to have a CT and he was a perfect patient. Of course the CT showed everything was normal. The only thing to do now is to wait until Monday to make an appointment with a GI doctor. We made this appointment and the doctor put my son on medication for GERD. Three weeks went by and still my son was in excruciating pain daily and vomiting weekly, so the GI doctor gave him pain medication. He felt even sicker after taking that medication, so we discontinued that med after two days. My thought is maybe a HIDA scan is the answer. A HIDA scan will show us if his gallbladder is functioning correctly, making his body think it's eating when in fact you have to fast the night before. After researching the procedure my son said there is no way he would be able to sit for 2 hours in this device lying still with loud noise and being hungry. I reluctantly agreed with him. At this point, we are at our wits end so I decided to start doing TAT sessions on my son, daily.

Our energy healer recommended I get intouch with with this healer from the UK who theories with Quantum K, so I emailed him and begged him for help. Between their help and the TAT sessions, we found out my son's gut pain was all emotional pain from childhood trauma. He was able to help my son with several energy healing, and much more. I put his contact information in the Resources chapter. After working with him my son found his bravery to confront and communicate with the individual regarding his childhood trauma. Even though this individual didn't acknowledge my son's trauma, my son kept his power and knew telling this individual about the past was healing himself. That his gut hurt was from past childhood trauma and it will get healed soon after speaking the "TRUTH". That the truth will prevail! Two weeks after his talk with this individual, my son's gut is almost 100% healed. I do have him on herbal pills for liver and immune support to help in aiding the physical body with recovery and I will do this for 3 months to make sure he is 100% healed, as well as a follow up appointment with this healer to ensure all our work is complete with this childhood trauma.

When my son has gut pain now, it is from an emotion, usually from fear. This gut pain could be daily or weekly and is a different gut pain then what is mentioned above. This gut pain is readily resolved with a TAT session. My son will tell me he has gut pain and I ask if he is feeling something, and he usually says "Yes, a fear of me (mom) getting into a car accident", or "Yes, I'm sad that…". We will then do a TAT session to remove the emotion that is causing the pain and he feels better instantly. Everyone has emotions and different physical reactions to these emotions. With doing TAT you will become more aware of your physical reaction and how to resolve any emotion/feeling, good or bad. For me, when I do a TAT session I may tear up, or have "heart ache". These emotions and /or feelings will usually be resolved within that TAT session. If whatever I'm working on is more serious, like a past trauma, it will take me a couple more TAT sessions. TAT will help with PTSD, weight loss, aggressive behavior, building confidence, having abundance and ease, and many more struggles and/or positive things you may face or want to bring into your life.

For my son to have the courage to approach this individual was something most children only dream of doing. Speaking the truth freed my son of this emotional and physical pain that he had been going through. My understanding of energy healing and working with my son daily, truly turned my world around. I used to solely blame vaccines on my son's diagnosis. Finding "victory" in blaming someone/something for my loss. The blame game has ended for me, I'm rejuvenated, and have NO more thoughts that "I made him Autistic". I do not have any more guilt as a parent and I certainly don't have that kind of power to make him autistic. I truly believe working with our own energy and our past lives, we can heal ourselves emotionally and physically.

Seeing it first hand with my son has made me realize his diagnosis was inevitable. His soul wanted and needed to come into this world to be complete. His soul's gift is to tell the truth. His diagnosis was a collaboration of things and events that made my son go into the abyss, including his soul giving up. My son has several gifts from God, and being a "star soul" is one of them. I truly believe he has found his courage, starting with telling his individual about the trauma he created, and knowing that telling the truth is much, much more important to his soul and the world.

For my son to relive the past over several years to create such physical pain, then to do energy clearing daily to try to overcome it, is in my opinion the most courageous thing a 17 year old could do. I am so very proud of him. Of course the secret is being courageous and incorporating energy healing into your life. No matter which modality you use I'm confident that energy healing will work for you. I encourage you to give it a try and see it changes your life. What have you got to lose?

Dr. Bradley Nelson said it best, "We are not physical bodies. Instead, a body is more like a temple that houses your spirit-self"[4]. In his book he explains emotions, trapped emotion codes, physical ailments, magnet healing, etc. This is how my son was able to heal his gut pain and trapped emotions. Dr. Nelson does go into detail as to how you remove these trapped emotions yourself and how to live a better life. Another great read is Energy Medicine by Donna Eden with David Feinstein, Ph.D[5]. This incredible woman healed her health ailments completely with energy healing and has devoted her life to helping others do the same. She talks about overcoming despair through spiritual connection and healing your body through these easy exercises you can do in your daily life to be healthy and happy. Showing you how to restore your energies, escaping the grip of fear, calming the nervous system, working on your rhythms, restoring peace after a bad dream, and many more issues we deal with on a day to day basis. I highly recommend getting this book or going to her website and joining her courses. You won't regret it.

---

[4] The Emotion Code by Dr. Bradley Nelson
[5] Energy Medicine by Donna Eden

10
Call to Action

Since this world has only made small adjustments for us, I feel we need to step up, come together, and make changes ourselves. I am asking everyone and anyone who wants these changes to happen to join/help me with this journey that I feel is greatly needed. I want to know what families need to make this world a safe and happy place for our special needs children. I wrote this book to help families with special needs. For parents, siblings, Aunts, Uncles, etc and to feel they have support.

Someone once said it takes a village to raise a special needs child. Well, I think we should build that village. A community where there is no bullying, no one feeling all alone or helpless. Love, peace, and harmony, compassion, understanding, where everyone helps each other and not judges one another. I want to give hope to other families, not despair. We shouldn't feel we are in this alone, because we are not. Not having someone trying to rip you off because the word autism/special need is attached to the sentence. I don't want families feeling alone, ashamed, or guilty in any way. I want there to be help for new parents giving birth or new diagnosis of any special needs, as well as every special needs child/adult from young to old to feel validated and most of all LOVED.

I believe in my gut that I'm not the only person thinking there has to be a change. I'm calling on all individuals who want to make a better/safer place for their children. I'm calling on all individuals who can make a contribution to help this community and anyone who has a voice that wants to be heard. Anyone that has a trade and would like to volunteer their time and knowledge or anyone who has materials that they would like to donate and/or anyone who has land. There are so many people who are so diverse and have so much knowledge that this community needs. We need to put our brains together and make this community happen for the sake of all involved and our future children. I know there are so many more treatments, modalities, experiences to share and learn. Whether you believe in Eastern or Western medicine, or both, we need to have a place where we feel our opinions/voices are being heard. A safe community for our children/adults. We can make a difference in our children's lives! I know we can do this. If you would like to participate in this amazing intentional community I am asking for your assistance now. If you want to fill out this survey in chapter 11 or just have any questions or ideas please contact me (see "Reference" chapter). My vision is a community where we all can share opinions and strive to make this world a better place for our children.

My daughter and son mean the world to me and they deserve an amazing life surrounded by people who have the same goals; to love, respect, and care about one another. My children have taught me so much and I thank God for them every day. I'm hoping and wishing we can build this community with amazing people.

Survey

If any of you would like to be a part of this community and you feel you have an opinion or desire to make things better and would like to contribute in any way, I'm asking that you complete this survey on my website so we can make your wishes and aspirations come true. Please feel free to contact me with your thoughts and ideas. My contact information is in the Resources chapter.

1) What would make your life easier for your child/adult?
2) If there was a special needs community what would you like it to consist of?
3) Hospitals: What would you need in order to have a successful visit?
4) Doctors offices: What would you need in order to have a successful visit?
5) Schools: What would you need in order for your child/adult to succeed?
6) SSI: What would you like to see change with this system?

7) Respite Care: What would make it easier for you?
8) Bullying: What would need to happen for repeat bullying?
9) Healthy foods in school? Yes/No and which ones. Which bad foods should stay?
10) Adult Programs: what type should there be?
11) Driving classes: Do we need them? Do we need practice roads?
12) Job Opportunities: What is needed in order to get them ready and to succeed?
13) Babysitting: What kind of system should be in place to give parents a break? Swap?
14) Social skills/Play dates/Activities/Parks/Support groups how would these run smoothly?
15) What would you like to see specifically changed about this world in order to help your special needs son/daughter?
16) What would you like to have weekly to help you with taking care of your child/adult?
17) What would you like to see schools offer for your child/adult?
18) How much care/help would you need per week for your situation?
19) What would you like to see colleges/advocate programs offer your son/daughter?
20) What sensory items have worked or not worked for your son/daughter?
21) What modality has worked best for your son/daughter? Whether in the past or currently?
22) Comments/things you would like to add or questions you would like to answer too?

23) What support systems need to be in place for special needs parents with a diagnosis or not, at any age?

24) What would've helped you become educated as a new parent?

25) What would've helped you when your son/daughter was diagnosed?

26) What should pedestrians offer to parents with new diagnosis?

27) What would help you and your family with your daily lives?

28) What types of holistic approaches would you like to share that have helped your son/daughter at any age?

29) Is there anything one book, podcast, ted talk, medical professional, medication, supplements, alternative treatment, therapy, modalities, training, etc that helped you out tremendously that you would like to share with the world to help other families?

30) Why did these treatments help?

31) What if any, modality helped a sibling through a diagnosis/disability? If nothing is out there for them, what would you like to see for our future children?

32) What Continuing education program/training was helpful and why?

33) What would you like to see change specifically at health care offices?

Resources

Michelle Mandolene
Email: michelle.mandolene@gmail.com
Web: www.michellemandolene.com
Facebook: Michellemandolene

Mark/Suzanne Solomon
Email: ConsultWithMark@yahoo.com
Web: SNFGuidance.com
Facebook: Financial guidance for a special needs families

Energy Healing
ACEP, the Association for Comprehensive Energy Psychology.
Web: www.energypsych.org

BioMagnetism
They don't have a directory of practitioners.
Web: www.biomagnetismusa.com

Our Healer
Integrative Relational Energetics
Web: www.ireinst.com. For individual work, classes for individuals and professional certification in Energy Psychology.

Somatic Therapy/Occupational Therapist
Patti Iwer, OTR/L, CST/2, Certified ScarWork Therapist,
Reiki Practitioner
Email: wellnessrising@gmail.com
Web: www.wellness-rising.com

Donna Eden
Web: www.edenmethod.com

Dr. Sears
Dr. Sears Alternative Vaccine Schedule-Naturopathic Pediatrics
Web: www.naturopathicpediatrics.com

Letterboard/keyboard typing
Web: www.halo-soma.org

Quantum K
Andrew Kempleton
Web: www.KempKinesiology.co.uk

Transcranial Magnetic Stimulation
Web: www.hopkinsmedicine.org

Tapas Acupressure Technique
Web: www.tatlife.com

Emotional Freedom Technique
Web: www.thetappingsolution.com

Transcendental Meditation
Web: www.tm.org

Books

Energy testing/muscle testing: The two books I found to be extremely helpful for me are:

Energy Medicine by Donna Eden and David Feinstein, Ph.D
Emotion Code by Dr. Bradley Nelson

Ido in Autismland, Climbing out of Autism's Silent Prison by Ido Kedar

Understanding Autism through Rapid Prompting Method by Soma Mukhopadhyay

Smart Medicine for a Healthier Child, 2nd edition by Janet Zand, N.D., L.Ac., Robert Rountree, M.D., Rachel Walton, MSN, CRNP

Printed in the United States
by Baker & Taylor Publisher Services